Ants at Work

Written by Michèle Dufresne

PIONEER VALLEY EDUCATIONAL PRESS, INC.

Here are some ants.

There are many kinds of ants.

They live **together** with other ants

in **colonies**.

Ants live in a home called a nest.

Some nests are made of sand

or twigs. Ants also make nests

in logs or in the **ground**.

Many ant nests have long tunnels and rooms called chambers. The chambers provide a place for ants to store food, rest, and care for young.

Ants have one **queen**. There are many **worker** ants. These ants make the nest, find **food**, and keep the nest safe.

4

There are also some
male ants. These ants are called
drones. The drone has one job,
to mate with the queen.

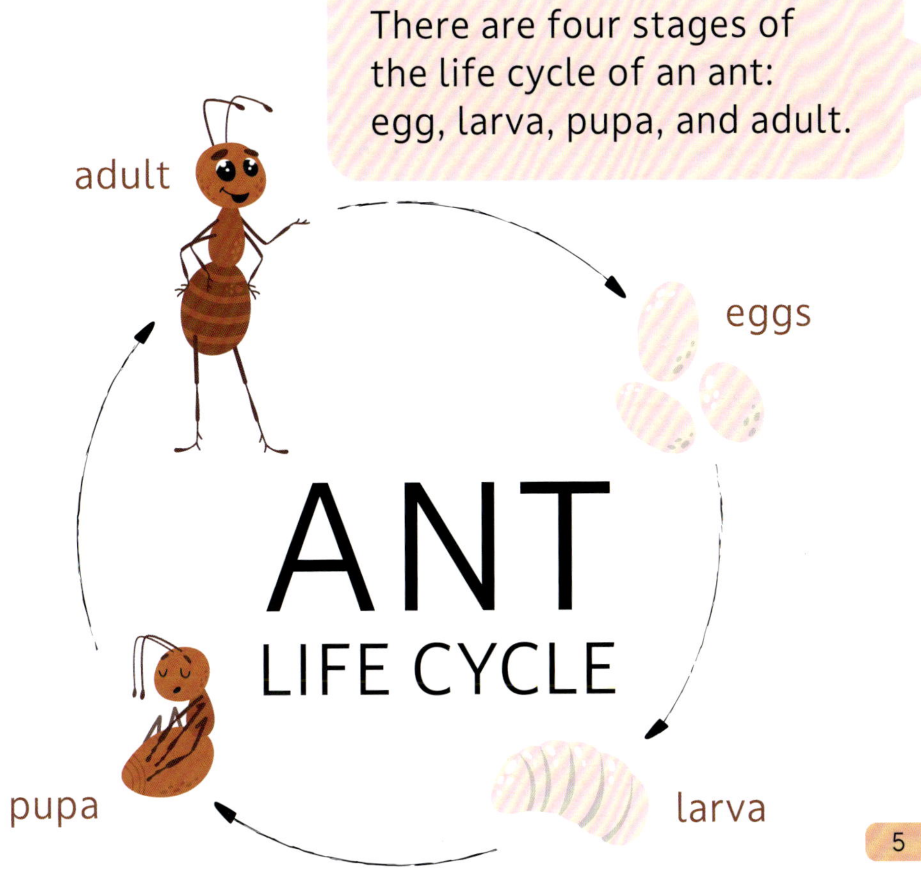

Ants are brave. They will bite and sting **predators** to save ants in the nest.

Ants are small but strong. They can lift things ten times their size!

An ant's strength comes from its muscles, despite its small size. Its body is built to carry heavy loads relative to its weight.

Ants **work** together all the time.
When an ant finds some food,
it will make a line of smells back to
the nest. The worker ants use
the smell to go back to the food.

This scent trail is made of chemicals called pheromones. Pheromones help ants communicate and guide each other to food sources.

Ants also work together to move big things. They move big bits of food back to their nest.

Ants often work together to move big pieces of food or objects. By teaming up, they can carry things much too heavy for one ant alone. This teamwork helps the whole colony.

glossary

colonies:
groups of
insects that
live together

food:
something
animals eat
to stay alive
and strong

ground:
the top layer
of the earth

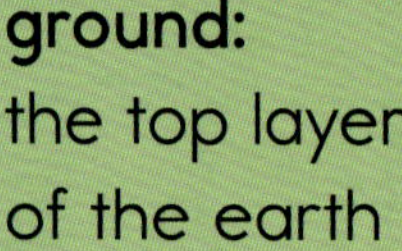

predators:
animals that
hunt and eat
other animals

queen:
the ant that
lays eggs in
the nest

together:
when two or
more animals
do something at
the same time
or as a group

work:
to do a job
or task

worker:
an ant that
does jobs like
finding food,
caring for eggs,
and building
the nest